Ramadan

M. C. Hall

Little World Holidays and Celebrations

ROURKE
PUBLISHING

www.rourkepublishing.com

www.rourkepublishing.com

Photo credits: Tjui Tjioe/iStockphoto, cover; Amrul Isham Ismail/Shutterstock Images, 3; Danish Khan/iStockphoto, 4; Vladimir Melnik/Shutterstock Images, 5; Wael Hamdan/iStockphoto, 6; Mahmoud Rahhal/iStockphoto, 7; Damir Cudic/ iStockphoto, 8; Erkki Makkonen/iStockphoto, 1, 9; David Smith/iStockphoto, 10; Jacek Chabraszewski/Shutterstock Images, 11; R Gombarik/Shutterstock Images, 12; Péter Gudella/Shutterstock Images, 13; Joe Biafore/iStockphoto, 14; Burak Pekakcan/iStockphoto, 15; Jeremy Richards/Shutterstock Images, 16; Rahmat Gul/AP Images, 17; Karen Moller/ iStockphoto, 18; Nasser Ishtayah/AP Images, 19; Ruslan Gilmanshin/iStockphoto, 20; Aman Khan/iStockphoto, 21

Editor: Holly Saari

Cover and page design: Kazuko Collins

Content Consultant: Suleiman Darrat, Doctorate of Engineering, Senior lecturer of Islamic studies, Department of Modern & Classical Languages, Literatures and Cultures, University of Kentucky

Library of Congress Cataloging-in-Publication Data

Hall, Margaret, 1947-
Ramadan / M.C. Hall.
   p. cm. -- (Little world holidays and celebrations)
Includes bibliographical references and index.
ISBN 978-1-61590-241-5 (hard cover) (alk. paper)
ISBN 978-1-61590-481-5 (soft cover)
1. Ramadan--Juvenile literature. I. Title.
BP186.4.H34 2011
297.3'62--dc22
                                        2010009915

16.⁰⁰

Rourke Publishing
Printed in the United States of America, North Mankato, Minnesota
033010
033010LP

www.rourkepublishing.com - rourke@rourkepublishing.com
Post Office Box 643328 Vero Beach, Florida 32964

What are these people doing?

They are celebrating Ramadan. Muslims around the world celebrate this holiday.

Muslims are people who practice the **religion** of Islam.

Ramadan remembers the time long ago when the Prophet Muhammad received the first **revelation** of the **Koran**.

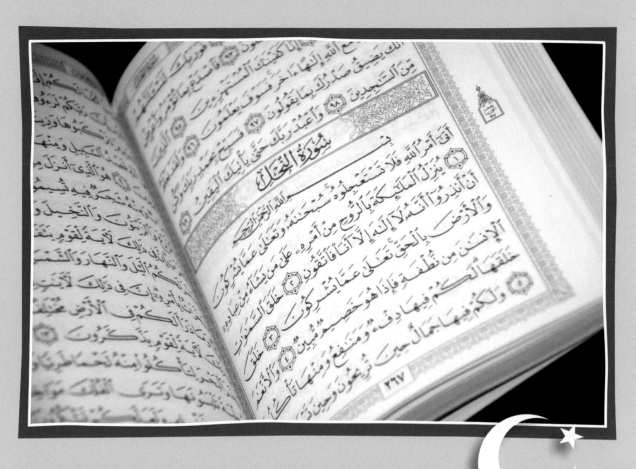

The Koran is the Muslim holy book.

Muslims use a calendar based on the Moon. The calendar has 12 months. Ramadan is the ninth month.

The holiday starts the day after the new moon can be seen. Ramadan lasts for one month.

Each day of Ramadan starts the same way.
Muslims eat a light meal before the Sun comes
up. Then they say a prayer.

Most adult Muslims **fast** during Ramadan. They do not eat or drink anything all day long. It is a joyful time for them.

During the month of Ramadan, many Muslims go to **mosques** more often. They read the Koran and pray together.

When the sun goes down, it is time to stop fasting and eat.

Muslims often start this meal by eating **dates**.

Then families have dinner together. The next day, they will fast again.

When Ramadan ends, there is a big celebration. It is called Eid-al-Fitr.

Eid-al-Fitr lasts for three days. It is a time for giving thanks.

People say prayers during Eid-al-Fitr. Then families and friends visit each other and share special meals.

During Eid-al-Fitr, Muslims help others. If a Muslim family has five members, then they have to feed five people who do not have enough to eat.

This holiday is also a time for fun. There are fireworks and music. Adults give gifts to children.

Ramadan and Eid-al-Fitr are very special celebrations for Muslims.

Recipe: Stuffed Dates

What you need:
- 20 pitted dates
- 20 whole almonds
- knife

1. With the help of an adult, cut a slit in each date.

2. Place an almond into each date's slit. It's okay if the almonds poke out of the dates.

3. Place the stuffed dates on a tray. Share the treat with your family!

Glossary

dates (DAYTS): sweet, sticky, brown fruits that grow on palm trees

fast (FAST): to choose to go without food or water for a certain amount of time

Koran (kor-AHN): the book of holy writings in Islam; also spelled Qur'an

mosques (MOSKS): buildings where Muslims pray and study their religion

religion (ri-LIJ-uhn): a system of belief, faith, and worship of God or gods

revelation (rev-uh-LAY-shuhn): something that God shows to humans

Websites to Visit

www.crayola.com/crafts/ramadan-(at-sundown)-crafts/

www.muslimkidsville.com/

www.primarygames.com/holidays/ramadan/coloring.htm

About the Author

M. C. Hall is a former elementary school teacher and an education consultant. As a freelance writer, she has authored teacher materials and more than 100 books for young readers. Hall lives and works in southeastern Massachusetts.